The Story
that matters

What is important in life?

Does this life lead to another li

Good answers to these questions
called the Holy Bible. To explain
will start at the very beginning of the story.

The word *Bible* is an ancient word which means 'book'.

The word *holy* means 'one of a kind'.

When we talk about the Holy Bible, we are talking about
a special, one-of-a-kind book. There are no other books
like the Bible. It is holy.

The Bible talks about many gods, but it only calls one
of these gods 'holy'. This God is different from all other
gods. He is very special. He is one of a kind.

People have names like Bill, Suzan, Ravi and Nishika. In
the same way, this special God has a name. His name
is Yahweh.

Because Yahweh is such a special God, people in the
past stopped using his name. Instead, they called him
Lord. This is what you call someone who is important—
someone who has authority. Although the Lord Yahweh
is a great God, he still wants to be friends with ordinary
people. He wants us to know all about him.

1

That is the reason God gave us the Bible. It is an important letter from Yahweh, which he wrote to all of us.

Yahweh wrote the letter many years ago. Yet, what it has to say is just as important today as when he wrote it. We all need to know what the Bible says to us.

The first pages in the Bible tell us that Yahweh was never born and he will never die. Yahweh had no beginning and has no end. This God has always existed and will always be. This is just one thing that makes him so special—one of a kind.

The Bible says that, in the beginning, there was only God. There were no plants, animals or people. There was no earth, moon or sun. There were no other gods. Nothing!

In the beginning, only the Lord Yahweh existed.

The Bible says that God made all the things we can see and all the things we cannot see.

One of the first things Yahweh did was to make angels. We cannot see angels, just as we cannot see God. Both angels and God are what we call *spirits*. They are like people, but they do not have bodies of skin and bone.

Although the angels are spirits, they are not gods. They are not the same as Yahweh. God made angels to be his special servants. They were to do whatever Yahweh asked.

All the angels watched and sang as God made the world.

The Bible says that when God created the world, he did it in an extraordinary way. When we make things, we need pencils and paper. Sometimes we use wood, nails and glue. However, the Bible says that when Yahweh made the world, he did not use any tools at all. God just spoke—and there it was!

God said, 'Let there be light'! Just like that, light appeared in the darkness.

Yahweh made everything we see merely by speaking words with his mouth. God has so much power—he can do anything! He is one of a kind! He is holy.

The Bible tells us that God made the sun, moon and stars. He placed them in the sky right where he wanted them. God could do that because he is everywhere.

It is good to know that God is everywhere. He is with you, your family and friends all at the same time. This is true no matter how far away they go or where they live.

Because Yahweh is everywhere at the same time, he even knows the thoughts we think. He knows and understands all things. We can never hide from God.

When we look at what Yahweh created, we see just how big and great the Lord God is.

The Bible says that God made the world in 6 days. Only the Lord Yahweh could do that.

He made the food we eat, the air we breathe and the water we drink. He made the rivers, seas and mountains. God made all the trees and flowers.

God made the fish that swim in the sea, as well as the birds that fly in the sky. He also made the animals we see in the forest and on the farm.

Last of all, God made people—both man and woman. The Lord loved them and looked after them.

He made a perfect garden. God filled it with all kinds of trees, flowers and tame animals. He did this especially for them. God wanted people to enjoy all that he had made.

When we look at the wonderful world God made, we can see that Yahweh is very powerful. He knows how to do everything. Only a great God could make the world we live in.

Since the Lord Yahweh made everything, he also owns everything. When you make something, you own it because you made it. It is the same way with God. Because God made everything, it all belongs to him. This is another reason why we call Yahweh, Lord. It means that he is the King and he owns all that he has made.

God created it, so he owns it.

The Bible tells us that Yahweh is good and kind.

Just look at all the beautiful things the Lord created. God could have made all flowers to be black and white, but instead he made them in pretty colours.

God could have made all food to taste awful. Instead, he made it good to eat and it smells great. He made all kinds of fruits and flowers, insects and animals, colours and sounds—just so we could enjoy them.

Yahweh did this because he cares for us.

The Bible says that God loves us.

The Bible also tells us that Yahweh likes things done in a right way.

Think how confusing it would be if the sun set one afternoon and did not rise again for 3 days. That is why God made rules. He made a rule for the sun—it was to rise in the morning and go down in the evening. It was to do that every day without changing. God made rules for everything he created, so that the world would work in the right way.

God made rules for people too. Sometimes we do not like rules. However, just stop and think for a moment what the world would be like without them. Driving your car would be dangerous if there were no stop signs. With no rules telling us what side of the road to drive on, everyone would be confused. Without rules, our lives would be very difficult.

The Lord God made rules because he knows what is best for us. He knows that when we do things in a right way, we are happy and safe. This is just another way Yahweh shows his love for us.

The Bible says that when God made the world, everything was perfect—there was nothing wrong with it. It was good in every way. The Lord Yahweh created a perfect world, because that is the way he is. He never does anything wrong. He is perfect.

God's home is also perfect. We call it *Heaven*. The Bible tells us that Heaven is very beautiful. It is like an enormous park with trees and a river. Right in the middle of this park is a beautiful, safe city. This city is so wonderful, God even made the streets out of gold.

In Heaven, there is no illness, pain or death. There are no weeds or poisonous plants. In Heaven nothing is ever broken or wears out. No bad or unkind people live there and everyone is always happy. Heaven is full of beautiful music. The animals are tame and friendly. You never have to sleep in Heaven, because there is no darkness or night. It is always day.

Heaven is a perfect place where perfect people and perfect angels live with a perfect God. Heaven is so wonderful, it is hard to describe.

After Yahweh finished making his perfect earth, something terrible happened. God's most important angel became unhappy.

This angel's name was Lucifer, which means the *Shining One*. God had created him to do a special job. However, Lucifer began to think he deserved something better. He did not want to be an angel any longer. He wanted to be in authority. Lucifer decided that he deserved to be God!

Since he did not want to follow God's rules, Lucifer made his own rules. He talked many other angels into fighting against Yahweh. They wanted to ruin everything, which made Heaven a very unhappy place.

The Bible uses a special word to describe Lucifer's choice to go against God. The Bible calls this *sin*. To sin means to decide not to follow God's rules. When you do this, you are telling the Lord that you think you know better than he does. Sin spoils things and it always hurts somebody.

We know this is true when we see a person carry out a crime or disobey a law. It hurts somebody. If officials catch the criminal, they punish him. He has to pay money or go to prison. That is only fair. It is not right for people to be wicked and somehow avoid punishment.

In the same way, the Bible tells us that God is always fair. He does not like it when people sin. He knows that sin always hurts someone. He punishes all sin with just the right amount of punishment. It is never too little and never too much. Yahweh always does that which is right and fair.

Lucifer and his angels hated God and did not want to obey him. Because Yahweh is perfect, he could not have these bad angels living with him in his perfect home. They were spoiling Heaven. Therefore, God threw them out and told them never to come back. God changed Lucifer's name to *Satan*, which means 'enemy'. Satan was now an enemy of God.

God made a new home for Satan and these bad angels. Because these angels were terrible, this new home was terrible. Because these angels were cruel and unhappy, this new home was a place of hurt and despair. This new home was an awful place called the Lake of Fire.

Those who live in this home, live there *forever*. It is a place of punishment for Satan and his bad angels.

Many angels followed Satan in choosing to *disobey* God. However, a lot more angels kept on obeying God and being his special servants. These good angels live with God and serve him in Heaven—Yahweh's perfect home.

The Bible says that in the beginning when God made the world, it was like Heaven. There were no tears, pain or fear. There were no bad or unkind people. No one stole, lied or killed. There was no sin of any kind. Best of all, nothing ever died.

The world God made was a wonderful place to live. It was the way God wanted things to be.

It was perfect.

The people God created were also perfect. Only perfect people can live with a perfect God.

The first man was named Adam and his wife was called Eve. Yahweh placed them in the beautiful garden he had created.

God allowed Adam and Eve to go anywhere they wanted. They could eat anything they liked, with one exception. God told them not to eat the fruit from one particular tree.

If Adam and Eve did not obey that one rule, it would be sin. If they chose to sin, they would not be able to live with Yahweh.

Following this rule was not difficult for Adam and Eve. There were plenty of fruit trees in the garden. However, by obeying God, Adam and Eve showed the Lord Yahweh that they believed him. They trusted that he knew what was best. This is what God wanted.

Yahweh was saying, 'Trust Me'.

That is how it was in the beginning—perfect people trusting a perfect God in a perfect world.

Then Satan came to the beautiful garden. He told Adam and Eve that Yahweh was hiding something good from them. Satan said that if they ate the fruit from that one tree, then they would be like God.

Was Satan telling the truth—or was he lying to them? What should Adam and Eve do? If they believed Satan, they would eat the fruit. However, if they believed God, they would not. Whom should they believe—Yahweh or Satan? Whom should they trust?

Adam and Eve began to think that being perfect people in God's perfect garden was not good enough. They wanted more. They wanted to be like Yahweh. Therefore, they did the one thing that God told them not to do—they ate the fruit.

Adam and Eve believed Satan's lie. They thought Satan knew better than God did what was good for them. They disobeyed God's one easy rule and joined with Satan against Yahweh.

This was sin.

Because of Adam and Eve's sin, the whole world changed. It was not safe and perfect like before. Just living became hard work. Weeds grew out of the ground. The animals started to kill each other. The world became a frightening place. Because of sin, the world was full of disease and despair. It became a place of death.

Adam and Eve thought that they were choosing what was best. However, their decision to disobey God ruined everything. The Bible says that death came into the world because of Adam and Eve's sin.

Death is an awful thing. When a person dies, his spirit leaves his body never to return. He will not live on earth again. That is why when we go to a funeral, we are sad. Our friend has left us and we feel all alone; death has separated us from each other.

In the same way, when Adam and Eve joined Satan's side, their sin separated them from Yahweh. The friendship was over and Adam and Eve felt all alone. That is what the Bible means when it talks about death. Sin has separated us from God.

Sin always spoils things—it ruined God's perfect world. It destroyed the special friendship Yahweh had with Adam and Eve.

However, that is not all. Because they had joined Satan, when their bodies died they would have to go and live in Satan's terrible home. Adam and Eve would have to remain forever in the Lake of Fire! This was such sad news, the Bible calls this the Second Death.

However, God did not want Adam and Eve to live with Satan. God loved Adam and Eve, but they could not live in Heaven. Only perfect people can live in Heaven. They had chosen to be sinful people by believing Satan. What would God do?

God was not without a solution! He had a plan. He told Adam and Eve just a little of his plan and what they heard was good news.

God promised to send a special man to earth. The Bible calls this man the *Saviour*. He would be able to save

Adam and Eve from the punishment for their sin. He could save them from the Second Death.

God did not tell how the Saviour would rescue Adam and Eve and make them perfect again.

However, he had promised a way. Would Adam and Eve believe God this time?

Would they trust him?

It is important to understand what the word *trust* means.

Let me explain. Let me tell you a story.

One day, John's *Grandpa* took him for a walk along the river. John got too close to the edge of the river and he slipped. Into the water he went! He struggled to the surface as the current swept him away. John was so afraid. The water was freezing cold. Because his clothes were wet and heavy, he felt himself sinking.

Then Grandpa stepped into the rushing water. He was a strong man and his feet were firm on the ground.

With his long arms reaching out to John, Grandpa shouted, 'Here! Take my hand; I will save you. Just trust me'!

What should John do? If he believed his grandfather, then he would grasp Grandpa's hand. If he did not believe his grandfather, then John would have to struggle on his own. It was Grandpa or himself.

Whom should he trust?

John reached out and took Grandpa's hand. He believed that his grandfather would save him from drowning. John made the right decision.

This was the choice God wanted Adam and Eve to make. He wanted them to trust him, believing that he would rescue them from Satan's terrible home.

Yahweh had a rescue plan, but Adam and Eve would have to trust him.

The Lord Yahweh did not tell Adam and Eve everything about his plan, or everything about the Saviour. However, he had made a promise. If people would trust God, then when they died, God would make them perfect. Perfect people can live with God in Heaven. All they needed to do was to trust God and believe his promise. It was that simple.

However, there was still one big problem. God could not make Adam and Eve perfect and let them go to Heaven without doing something about their sin. Adam and Eve had joined Satan's side and had become sinful. God could not pretend that this had never happened. To refuse to notice their sin would not be right or fair. God must punish all wrong.

So, how could God punish Adam and Eve's sin without punishing them?

This is an important question. You see, we are all like Adam and Eve. We have sin that needs punishment. Since we all sin, we need to know how God can punish sin without punishing people.

To help us understand, God explained a little bit more of his plan.

Because people did not understand how bad sin was, God asked them to do something that would help them understand. This would show them how he would punish sin without punishing people.

Yahweh told them to select an animal—a *lamb*. It must be a male lamb and it could not have anything wrong with it. It could not be sick or have any injuries. It had to be perfect.

God explained that they were to bring the lamb to an altar, a special place of death. The one bringing the lamb was to put his hand on the lamb's head. In doing this, God said it would be like placing all the man's sin on the lamb.

Now something sad had to happen.

Do you remember how death came into the world because of sin? Well, because the man had placed his sin on the lamb, the lamb had to die. This helped people understand that the man's sin had put the lamb to death.

God asked people to do this so that they could understand his plan. This is how he would punish sin without punishing people. The lamb suffered the punishment instead of the man.

The man did what God said because he trusted Yahweh. He believed that the lamb suffered his punishment.

When the time came for the man to die, God would make him perfect so he could live in Heaven.

This was God's plan. It was just one way he showed us how much he loved us.

However, some people did not believe God's plan.

They said there were other gods who were more important than Yahweh. They thought these gods had better plans.

What these people did not understand was that these gods were really Satan's bad angels. They were only pretending to be like Yahweh to deceive them. They were lying and not telling the truth.

It was not right that people should consider bad angels as more important than Yahweh. There is only one true God and people should listen to him. Only Yahweh tells the truth.

Even so, people were quite sure that Yahweh's plan could not be right. The idea of trusting God to make one perfect—that was too simple. They thought they needed to do something more, so they came up with their own plan. They made their own rules.

They said that if people did more good things than bad things, then God would be happy. If people were kind, then they would be good enough to live in a place like Heaven.

Do you know what? These people did not understand how good they would have to be to live with God in his perfect Heaven.

Therefore, Yahweh explained some things.

He said that if people stole something, no matter how little, then they were not good enough for Heaven.

Yahweh told them that if they loved money more than they loved him, then they were not perfect.

He said that if they did not control their anger, that was sin.

If they ever told a lie, even just a little lie, then they were not perfect. It was a sin to tell lies.

The Lord said that being unkind or not using God's name in an honourable way was sin.

Not showing respect to their mother or father, even just once, meant they were not perfect.

Only perfect people can live with a perfect God.

In total, God gave the people 10 rules called the 10 *Commandments*. The Lord wrote them on 2 flat stones. No one could add their own rules nor could they rub one out. God's rules never change.

The Lord gave the 2 stones to a man by the name of Moses. Moses was to show all the people what Yahweh had written.

Everyone needed to understand that, even if they tried very hard, they could never obey God's 10 rules entirely. They could never be good enough to live with God. They were sinful people. They could not save themselves from the punishment their sin deserved.

They needed a Saviour—they needed a lamb.

For many years, the people waited with hope for the Saviour's arrival.

At last, the day came. The Saviour arrived on earth! What was so surprising was that the Saviour was Yahweh himself. That is right—God came to earth. That is astonishing!

To be the Saviour, Yahweh became a man. This does not mean that he stopped being God. However, the Lord knew that the only way to save us was to become like us. For this reason he entered the world as a baby, just like any other child arrives on earth.

Yahweh was born into an ordinary family. His mother's name was Mary and her husband's name was Joseph. Although the family was ordinary, the baby was not. He was holy—one of a kind! The baby was God himself.

Yahweh was not born in a hospital. He was born in a stable—a place where sheep and lambs are kept warm.

His first visitors were shepherds—men who take care of lambs and keep them safe.

When God came to earth, his name was Jesus. Jesus means *Yahweh is the one who saves*.

Jesus was the Saviour whom God had promised to Adam and Eve many years ago. He came to save us from the punishment our sin deserves. This is one big reason why it is so important to know the story of the Bible. It is because we all need a Saviour.

The story of Yahweh coming to earth as a baby is still celebrated in many countries. Each year, on the 25th day of December, people gather for a special holiday called Christmas. At Christmas, friends give each other gifts to remind each other of God's great gift to us. God's gift was a Saviour.

But the story is not finished.

After Jesus became an adult, he began to do many extraordinary things. He made blind men see and cured those who could not walk. He healed many who were sick—some with terrible diseases like *leprosy*. Jesus even had power over death. He made people who had died alive again.

On one occasion, he fed a huge, hungry crowd. There were thousands of people and Jesus had only 5 loaves of bread and 2 fish. However, as men helped Jesus pass out the food, the bread and fish kept increasing! Everyone had enough to eat. When they were finished, they even gathered 12 baskets of extra bread.

All could see that Jesus loved people. Jesus did these things so everyone would know he was God.

One night, some of Jesus' friends decided to travel by boat across a big lake. While they were out on the water, they were caught in an awful storm. The wind was fierce and huge waves crashed against the boat.

All night the men tried to get the boat to shore, but the wind was too strong. Near dawn, the men could see someone walking on top of the water. They thought it was a ghost! They were frightened.

Then a voice called out to them, 'It is me, do not be afraid'. It was Jesus!

Peter shouted from the boat, 'Lord, if it is you, tell me to come to you on the water'.

Jesus said, 'Come'.

Peter got out of the boat. He began to walk to Jesus on top of the water.

However, when Peter looked at the wind and waves, he became afraid and began to sink. What should he do? He could struggle on his own, or he could call out to Jesus to save him. Whom should he trust?

Peter knew that he could not save himself; Jesus was the only one who could rescue him. He cried out, 'Lord, save me'! Jesus reached out his hand and caught Peter. Peter made the right choice.

In the same way that Peter could not save himself from drowning, we cannot save ourselves from sin's punishment. We need a Saviour.

The Bible says that Jesus is our Saviour. We need to trust him.

While on earth, Jesus lived like any other man. He worked as a carpenter and visited with friends. He ate, slept and travelled to many places. However, Jesus was also different from you and me. Jesus never did anything wrong.

All the time he lived on earth, even as a little boy, he never did one bad thing. Jesus was the only man who ever lived a perfect life. He was one of a kind.

Because Jesus lived a perfect life, he had no sin that needed punishment. He did not need to die. People only die because of sin and Jesus did not sin.

Although Jesus did not have to die, he told people that one day men would kill him. They would beat him, striking him many, many times with a whip. Then they would hammer huge nails through his hands and his feet to hang him on a wooden cross. Jesus would die. After being dead for 3 days, he would come back alive.

Those who heard him say this did not believe it. They told him not to talk that way, but what Jesus said was true. He told his friends the rest of God's plan; he told them good news.

It was all about God's promise—it was all about the lamb.

Do you remember the lamb?

Another name for Jesus was the Lamb of God.

Do you remember how the lamb had to be a male lamb?

Well, Jesus was a man.

The lamb also had to be perfect.

Jesus was perfect—he was without sin.

God told the man that he had to bring the lamb to an altar, a special place of death.

William on earth, Jesus allowed men to bring him to a cross, a special place of death.

Do you remember how the one bringing the lamb put his hand on the lamb's head? This showed that he placed his sin on the lamb.

The Bible says that as Jesus hung on the cross, he took all our sin on himself. He took the sin of everyone—from the best of people to the worst of men and women.

Jesus heard all the nasty words that people had ever said. He knew all the terrible things that people had ever done. He could see all the anger that people had ever shown. He felt all the hurt that people had ever caused. The perfect Jesus took all the awful effects of sin upon himself. He felt it all, he knew it all and he took it all. It must have been terrible.

Yes, it all had to do with a lamb.

Jesus was the Lamb—our Lamb.

Now think back to the rest of the story. Do you remember what happened to the lamb? Because God must punish sin and the punishment is death, the lamb had to die.

It was the same way with Jesus.

Because Jesus had taken all our sin onto himself, he must suffer the punishment. Jesus had to die.

The Bible says that Jesus died for us. He took all the punishment our sin deserved, so that we would never need to suffer the Second Death.

Jesus was the final Lamb; man did not need to bring any more lambs to an altar. Jesus had done it all.

The Lord Yahweh had kept his promise.

If the story ended with Jesus dead on the cross, it would be very sad.

However, the Bible tells us more. It says that after Jesus died, his friends took his body down from the cross. They put him in a special grave called a tomb. A tomb is like a cave—a small room cut in solid rock. Slowly, they rolled a big stone across the door. Then sadly, they turned and went home.

The next day, the men who had killed Jesus told soldiers to guard the tomb. They knew Jesus had said that he would rise from the dead after 3 days. They did not want anyone taking Jesus' body away and pretending he was alive. They wanted to make sure his body stayed dead in the tomb.

In spite of this, neither the soldiers nor the big stone could stop God. Nothing could stop God's plan. As Jesus had said, after 3 days, he rose from the dead! Jesus was alive!

44

An angel rolled back the stone so everyone could see that Jesus was not in the grave. Upon seeing the angel, the guards were so afraid they shook and became like dead men.

Later, when some women came to the tomb, the guards were gone. Only an angel remained to tell them what had happened. These women were the first to see Jesus. He was alive from the dead!

This part of the story is still celebrated in many countries. Each year, during the months of March or April, people gather for special days called Good Friday and Easter Sunday. On Good Friday they think about Jesus' death on the cross. On Easter Sunday they remember how Jesus' friends buried him in a tomb and how he rose from the dead. It is because he is alive that they can be so happy.

But the story is not finished.

For 40 days, Jesus met with his friends and large groups of people. Everyone was excited. He was talking, eating and travelling with them again. It was wonderful!

Jesus was alive!

People could hardly believe it. No one had ever done this before. No one had died and then brought himself back from the dead!

Jesus was showing them that because he was God, he was stronger than death. People did not need to be afraid of dying and going to the Lake of Fire. They did not need to be afraid of the Second Death. Jesus was strong enough to bring them back alive.

However, he would not bring them back to live on earth—a place that has been spoiled by sin.

Rather, he would take them to Heaven—a place that is perfect and full of happiness.

Jesus was promising to do this for all those who would trust him. It was that simple.

All people needed to do was believe that Jesus was their Lamb—that he took the punishment for their sin. They needed to trust Jesus, believing that what he said was true. Then, when they finished living here on earth, Jesus would make them perfect so they could live in Heaven.

This was true for all people from every nation, whether man, woman, boy or girl. Anyone who trusted Jesus could live forever in Heaven.

The people listened with excitement. This was news everyone needed to hear. They talked for long hours with Jesus about the plan. Then, after 40 days, Jesus said goodbye and returned to Heaven. That is where he lives now, in his perfect home.

Someday Jesus will return to this earth. But until then, Yahweh wants us to know that nothing is more important in life than to trust in Jesus as our Saviour.

Jesus said he is God Yahweh. Do you believe him?

Jesus said he died in your place for your sin. Do you believe that is true?

Jesus said he came back to life. Do you believe him?

If you believe Jesus—if you take God at his word—then he says you will live forever with him in Heaven. That is good news! That is what the Bible is all about. It is the story that matters.

Do you understand God's letter?

Yahweh's letter—the Holy Bible—is so important, you need to make sure you clearly understand it. Take some time to answer the following questions. They will help you discover how well you understand God's plan. If you get some of the questions wrong, read this book again until the answers are clear in your mind.

1. Why was God only able to create a perfect world?

2. The Bible uses a special word to describe Lucifer's choice to disobey God. What is that word?

3. Why is it wrong for someone to do bad things and not suffer punishment?

4. What is the name of the home that Yahweh created for Satan and the bad angels?

5. The Bible uses a word to describe Adam and Eve's choice to disobey God. What is that word?

6. What came into the world because of sin?

7. Because of their sin, Adam and Eve were not perfect. Therefore, when they died they would have to live with Satan in the Lake of Fire. What does the Bible call this sort of death?

8. God promised he would send a special man to rescue all people from the Second Death. What does the Bible call this man?

9. Why does God need to make people perfect in order for them to live in Heaven?

10. Could God pretend that Adam and Eve's sin had never happened?

11. God showed people how he would punish sin without punishing them. What sort of animal did God tell them to bring?

12. What happened to the man's sin when he put his hand on the head of the lamb?

13. For whom did the lamb die?

14. Since the lamb had not done anything wrong, why did it suffer punishment?

15. If people trust Yahweh, when they die they go to Heaven. How does God change them so they are able to live in his perfect home?

16. If we do good things all our lives, will we be good enough to live in Heaven?

17. Who left Heaven to become the Saviour?

18. Since Jesus was without sin, did he have to die?

19. The Bible says that Jesus was like the lambs that people brought to the altar. What name does the Bible give to Jesus that reminds us of those lambs?

20. The Bible says the lamb took the sin of the people. Whose sin did Jesus take on himself?

21. The lamb died instead of the man. For whom did Jesus die?

22. What do people need to do so that Jesus can take them to live in Heaven?

What you have read in this book is only a small part of what the Bible says about God's plan. The Bible is full of stories telling us how God can accept us.

See answers on page 54

Do you believe God's letter?

If you have answered all the questions right, it means you understand God's plan. To understand God's letter is very good, however, that is not enough. You need to make a decision. You see, it is one thing to understand the Bible; it is another thing to believe it.

Try answering these questions. They will help you to know if you believe God's letter.

1. When Yahweh came to live on the earth, did he stop being God?

2. Who is Jesus? Do you believe Jesus is Yahweh?

3. God is perfect. Are you perfect? Do you believe you are good enough for Heaven, or do you believe you are a sinner?

4. Do you believe that God will punish all sin?

5. Who took the punishment for your sin?

6. Do you believe that Jesus is your Lamb?

7. After Jesus died, he rose from the dead and now lives in Heaven. Do you believe that is true?

Did you give the right answers to these questions? Do you believe your answers to be true? If so, then the Bible says Jesus has paid the punishment for your sin. He is your Saviour. You will never have to be afraid of the Second Death or the Lake of Fire.

When you believe the Bible is true, it means you trust Yahweh. Because you trust him, God says you are his friend. He promises never to leave you. He will always be with you, no matter where you go or what you do.

When you finish living here on earth, God says he will make you perfect for Heaven. You will live with him forever. This is great news! It is something you can know for sure because God said it and God does not tell lies.

Perhaps this book has answered many questions for you. The Bible is full of this sort of information. In it you find the answers for how you should live your life every day. It would be good to get a Bible and start by reading the section called 'The Gospel of John'. Take some time to read the Bible each day.

There is one more important thing to say. When someone does something special for you, you thank him. The Bible says that you can talk to the Lord just like one friend talks to another. The Bible calls this prayer.

Here are some words to say 'thank you' to Jesus for what he did for you. You can pray and thank him in your own words. Remember God is everywhere—he is listening.

> Dear Jesus, I know you are God and you created all things. You are perfect; I am a sinner. You are the only one who can save me. I believe you died on the cross and took the punishment for my sin. I trust you as my Saviour. Thank you for loving me so much. I know you will keep your promise to take me to Heaven to be with you.

Yes, Jesus is a wonderful Saviour.

See answers on page 54

Answers: Do you understand God's letter?

1. He is perfect (page 8).
2. Sin (page 10)
3. It is not fair (or right). All wrong needs punishment (page 10).
4. The Lake of Fire (page 12)
5. Sin (page 18)
6. Death (page 18)
7. The Second Death (page 20)
8. A Saviour (page 20)
9. Only perfect people can live with a perfect God (page 24).
10. No (page 24)
11. A lamb (page 24)
12. The lamb took the man's sin (page 25).
13. For the man (page 26)
14. It had taken the man's sin (page 26).
15. He makes them perfect (page 27).
16. No (page 31)
17. God, Yahweh, Jesus—all the same (page 32)
18. No (page 40)
19. The Bible calls Jesus 'the Lamb of God' (page 41).
20. Our sin (page 42)
21. For us (page 43)
22. Trust him or believe him (page 47).

Answers: Do you believe God's letter?
It is your choice to decide what to say. We hope you answer this way.

1. No, he did not stop being God.
2. Jesus is God. Yes, Jesus is Yahweh.
3. I am a sinner.
4. Yes
5. God, Jesus
6. Yes
7. Yes, I believe it is true.

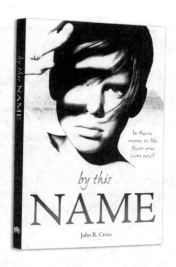

John R. Cross

Do not stop now!

What you have read is only a summary of what the Bible says about God's plan. For example, the connection you see between the lamb and Jesus is just one of many illustrations in the Bible. There are many others. Take the next step to learn more about who Jesus is and what he did on the cross.

To gain an even better understanding, read *By This Name.* This book will explain further God's plan to save everyone.

To find out more about *By This Name* and how to obtain a copy, go to this website:

www.goodseed.com

Continue your learning journey!

Bible Verses

The sentences below are from the EasyEnglish Bible. Available at: easyenglish.info

Pages 2 and 3

Isaiah 45:5 I am the Lord … Apart from me, no god exists.

Jeremiah 10:6 There is no one like you, LORD. You are great and your name is powerful.

Isaiah 40: 26,28 Look up at the sky! God created all the stars that you see … he knows exactly how many stars there are. Because God's power is so great, not one of them is ever missing … the Lord has always been God. It was he who created the world and everything in it. God never gets tired. He never wears himself out. No human being can fully (completely) understand God's ways.

Psalm 145:3 Clearly the LORD is great … We will never know how great he really is!

John 4:24 God is Spirit.

Hebrews 1:14 All the angels are spirits who work for God.

Psalm 103:20,21 Praise the LORD, you (who are) his angels. You are strong and powerful. You do what he tells you (to do) and you obey his word.

Pages 4 and 5

Hebrews 11:3 By our trust in God, we understand that he made the world by his word of command. He made all the things that we see out of things that do not appear.

Genesis 1:3 And God said, 'Let there be light.' And then there was light.

Jeremiah 32:17 Lord, king of all people, you have made the earth and the sky by your great power. Your hands have made them. Nothing is too difficult for you to do.

Genesis 1:16 And God made two great lights. The larger light ruled the day, and the smaller light ruled the night. God made the stars too.

Jeremiah 23:24 No one can hide in a secret place so that I cannot see him', says the Lord.

Genesis 1:1 In the beginning, God created the skies and the earth.

Exodus 20:11 In six days, the Lord made the sky, the earth and the sea. He also made everything that is in them.

Genesis 1:21 So God … created all the different creatures that move everywhere in the seas. He also created all the birds that fly in the sky.

Genesis 1:25 God made all kinds of wild animals on the earth. He made all kinds of cattle. And he made all kinds of creatures that crawl.

Genesis 2:7 Then the Lord God formed a man from dust that was on the earth.

Pages 6 and 7

Isaiah 44:24 The Lord says, 'I created you in the beginning. I am the Lord who made everything. I alone established the heavens. I alone created the earth. There was nobody else with me.

Psalm 24:1 The earth belongs to the LORD. Everything in it is his own. The world belongs to the LORD. Everybody in it is his own.

1 Timothy 6:17 … he [God] gives to us everything that we need to enjoy life.

Genesis 1:31 God saw everything that he had made. And it was really very good.

Deuteronomy 32:4 He is The Rock that is strong. It does not move away. His work is completely good. All the things that he does are fair. He is a God who keeps his promises. He never does anything that is wrong. He does what is fair and good.

Psalm 89:14 You have built your kingdom doing what is right and fair. Your kind love and the fact that you keep your promises go in front of you.

Page 8

Revelation 21:27 Only what is good and clean (holy) will be able to enter the city. Nobody who does awful things will ever go into it. Nobody who tells lies will be able to go in.

Revelation 21:3 God himself will be with them and he will be their God.

Revelation 21:10-12, 25 The city shone with the bright light that comes from God. It glowed like a precious stone … The city had a great, high wall with 12 gates in it … They will never close because there is no night there.

Revelation 21:21 The main street of the city was pure gold, as clear as glass.

Revelation 22:1 Then the angel showed me the river of the water that gives life. It shone like crystal.

Revelation 22:5 There will be no night there. They will not need the light of a lamp or the light of the sun. Instead, the Lord God will provide their light.

Revelation 21:4 He will wipe every tear from their eyes. Nobody will ever die again. Nobody will ever be sad again. Nobody will weep and nobody will suffer pain.

Page 10

1 John 3:4 All who sin are guilty. They have failed to do what the law demands. We sin when we fail to obey the law.

Isaiah 14:12-14 How you have fallen from the sky, you bright Morning Star! … Now you have suffered the same fate. God has chopped you to the ground, just as men cut down a tree. You proudly said to yourself, "… I shall be … like God Most High."

Proverbs 6:16-17 God opposes 6 things. In fact he hates 7 things: proud eyes, a mouth that speaks lies, hands that murder.

Ecclesiastes 12:14 Sometimes we do wrong things. We think that no one sees us. But God sees the things that we do. And he will ask us to explain the answer to this question. What have we done with our lives here on the earth?

Pages 12 and 13

Ezekiel 28:16-17 … I threw you down from God's mountain. Because of your sin, you, the special cherub, were not fit to be there … You were too proud because of your beauty. You ruined your wisdom because of your greatness. I threw you down to the earth.

Revelation 20:10 The devil will cause this war by his lies. Then the Lord will throw him into the lake of fire and sulphur … The fire and sulphur will punish all of them, day and night. It will never end.

Matthew 25:41 Go into the fire that burns for ever. God has prepared it for the devil and his messengers.

Pages 14 and 15

Genesis 1:27 So God created people so that they were like himself. He created people as his image. He created them as man and woman.

Genesis 2:15 The Lord God took the man. And he put the man in the garden that was in Eden.

Genesis 2:9 God made all the trees grow there that are pleasant to look at. And their fruit is good to eat. Also, in the middle of the garden, there were these two trees. There was the tree that makes people live. And there was the tree that makes people know right things and wrong things.

Genesis 2:16-17 The Lord God gave these orders to Adam. 'You can eat from all the other trees in the garden … But you must not eat fruit from the tree that makes you know right things and wrong things. You will die on the day when you eat that fruit. That is why you must not eat it.'

Pages 16 and 17

Genesis 3:1,4-5 The snake [which is Satan] said this to the woman: 'Did God say that you can eat the fruit from all the trees in the garden?' … But the snake replied to the woman, 'You will not die. But when you eat the fruit, your eyes will open. God knows that. You will be like God and you will know right things and wrong things.'

Pages 18 and 19

Genesis 3:6 So the woman saw that the fruit was good to eat … She also thought that it would make her wise. She then took some fruit and she ate it. She also gave some fruit to her husband and he ate it.

Genesis 3:19 You will sweat in order to grow food. That will happen until you die. And then people will bury you. I made you from the dust, and you will again be dust.'

Romans 8:22 We know how deeply everything suffers. Everything that God created is crying in pain right up to now.

Romans 5:12 Sin entered the world because one man sinned. And death came because of sin. Everyone sinned, so death came to all people.

Romans 6:23 When you sin, the only result of your efforts is death.

Isaiah 59:2 It is your own wicked lives that have separated you from your holy God. It is your evil deeds that have hidden God from you.

Colossians 1:21 You thought and behaved in an evil way. So you were God's enemies.

Pages 20 and 21

Revelation 21:8 But the future for many people will be in the lake that burns with fire and sulphur. This is the second death.

Isaiah 54:8 … with love without end I will take you back.' So declares the Lord your rescuer.

Isaiah 43:11 I alone am the Lord. I alone can rescue you in your present situation. And in the future.

Pages 22 and 23

Hebrews 11:1 Faith, that is, trust in God, is the foundation of what we hope for. It is being completely sure of what we do not yet see.

Hebrews 11:6 If a person does not trust in God, he cannot please him.

Psalm 27:1 The LORD is my light and he makes me safe. Who will make me afraid? The LORD is my hiding place. So, who will make me afraid?

Psalm 118:8 It is better to trust in the LORD than to trust in people …

Psalm 115:11 Everyone that is in awe of the LORD … trust in the LORD.

Pages 24 and 25

Romans 3:23 Everyone has sinned. Nobody is good enough because God's standards are perfect.

2 Samuel 14:14 One day we will all die. We are like water that spills on the ground. Nobody can gather it up again. However, God does not take away people's lives. Sometimes people separate themselves from God. But God's plan is always to bring people back to himself.

Leviticus 5:17-18 A person might do wrong things. But he might not know that they were wrong. He is sinning. When he knows about it, he must bring a sheep to the priest. The animal must be a perfect male.

Leviticus 1:4 The person must put his hand on the animal's head. Then he must kill it. The animal's death will pay for the person's sins.

Leviticus 5:17-18 Then the Lord will forgive the person.

Pages 26 and 27

Proverbs 3:5 Trust in God with your whole heart. Do not depend on your own intelligence!

Page 28

Exodus 20:23 Do not make any gods to be equal to me. Do not make for yourselves gods out of silver or out of gold.

Exodus 20:2-5 …You must not make any false god for yourself. Do not make a false god in the shape of anything in the sky. Do not make one in the shape of anything on the earth or in the water. You must not … worship it.

1 Corinthians 10:20-21 You cannot drink the cup of the Lord and the cup of demons as well. You cannot eat bread at the Lord's table and at the table of demons.

2 Corinthians 11:14 Even Satan himself pretends to be an angel of light.

Romans 1:24-25 They believed a lie instead of the truth about God. They chose to worship and to serve something that God created. But they ought to worship and to serve God himself, who created everything. He should receive honour always.

James 2:10 We must obey every rule that the law tells us. If we fail to obey one small rule, we have failed to obey the whole law.

Romans 3:20 And God will not declare anyone to be righteous because that person obeyed the law. Instead, the law proves that everyone has sinned.

Hebrews 4:12-13 No one can hide from God. His eyes see all things as they really are. It is to him that we all must give an account for what we do.

Pages 30 and 31

Exodus 20:12-16 Always be very kind to your father and your mother. Then you will live for many years in the country that the Lord will give to you. You must not murder anyone. You must not have sex with another person's husband or wife. You must not take another person's things for yourself. You must not say false things about your neighbour.

Exodus 24:12 The Lord said to Moses: 'Come up to me on the mountain. Stay here and I will give the flat stones to you. I have written on them the Law and the rules. So now you can teach them to the people.'

Pages 32 and 33

Psalm 130:5,7-8 I will wait for the LORD. I will wait for him and hope in his word …

Isaiah 9:6 A child has been born for us … His names will be 'Wonderful Adviser' and 'All-Powerful God'. And 'Father Always' and 'Commander-Who-Brings-Peace'.

Luke 2:7 She gave birth to her first son. Mary wrapped him in strips of cloth and laid him in an open box. This box usually held animals' food.

Luke 2:8-12 In that part of the country, not far from Bethlehem, there were shepherds out in the fields. They were looking after their sheep during the night. An angel of the Lord appeared to them. The glory of the Lord was shining over them. They were full of fear. But the angel said to them, 'Do not be afraid! I have come to give you good news. This will bring great joy to everybody. For today, a Saviour has been born for you in the city of David. He is Christ the Lord. This will be the evidence for you. You will find a baby wrapped in strips of cloth. He is lying in a place where animals have their food'.

Matthew 1:25 And Joseph gave him the name 'Jesus'.

Page 34

Matthew 4:23-24 Jesus went all over Galilee district. He taught the Jewish people in the houses where they met. And he explained the Good News to them. He urged them to choose God's rule. He also healed people who were suffering from every kind of illness and disease. News about him spread over the entire country called Syria. So people brought everyone who was ill or in pain to him. They were suffering from every kind of illness and disease … Jesus healed them all.

Matthew 14:14-21 And when Jesus landed, he saw a large crowd of people. He felt great sympathy for them. So he healed the people who where ill. When it was nearly evening, the disciples came to Jesus. 'There is nothing here', they said to him. 'It is already getting late, so you must send the crowds away. Then they can go and buy some food in the villages.' But Jesus replied to them. 'They do not need to go away', he said. 'You give them something to eat.' ' We have only five loaves of bread and two fish', they answered … Then he broke the loaves into pieces and he gave them to the disciples. Then the disciples gave the food to the people. All of them ate and had enough to eat. Afterwards, the disciples picked up 12 baskets full of broken pieces that the people had left. There were about 5000 men who ate the food. There were women and children who ate as well.

Page 37

Matthew 14:24-26,28-29 The boat with his disciples was already a long way from land. The boat was in difficulty because a strong wind was blowing against it. And the waves were very high. Very early the next morning, Jesus went out to the disciples on the lake. He walked on the water. The disciples saw him walking on the lake. Then they were very afraid. 'It's a ghost!' they screamed. They cried out because they were very afraid. 'Lord, if it is really you, talk to me. Tell me to come to you on the water', Peter said to him. 'Come', Jesus replied. So Peter got out of the boat and he walked on the water towards Jesus.

Pages 38 and 39

Matthew 14:30-31 But when Peter saw the wind, he was afraid. He began to sink in the water and he cried out to Jesus. 'Lord save me!' he called. Immediately, Jesus reached out his hand and caught Peter. 'You do not really believe me!' he said. 'There was no reason for you to doubt.'

Pages 40 and 41

1 Peter 2:22 'He (Messiah) did not sin. He did not say anything wrong'

Hebrews 7:25-27 Jesus does not need to make sacrifices every day ... He did not need to do this on his own behalf, for he was perfect and without sin.

Matthew 16:21 From that time on, Jesus began to explain to his disciples what would happen to him. 'I must go to Jerusalem', he told them. 'There, our nation's leaders, and the chief priests and the men who teach the Law will cause me to suffer many things. They will kill me. But on the third day I will be alive again.'

John 1:29 The next day, John the Baptist saw Jesus. Jesus was coming towards him. John the Baptist said, 'Look! This man is God's Lamb who takes away the sins of everyone in the world.

Pages 42 and 43

1 Peter 1:19 Instead God bought you with the precious blood of Christ. Christ was like a perfect lamb (young sheep) that the Jews sacrificed.

1 Corinthians 5:7 ... because Christ is our Passover lamb. He has become a sacrifice for us.

2 Corinthians 5:21 Christ did not do any sins. But God made Christ become sin instead of us. As a result, we can receive God's goodness by him.

Romans 3:25 God gave Jesus as a sacrifice so that people would receive a right relationship with himself. Jesus achieved this by the gift of his life (in other words, when he died for us). And people receive a right relationship with God by faith in what Jesus did.

Pages 44 and 45

John 19:41-42 There was a garden in the place where Jesus had died. There was a new grave in this garden. Nobody had ever used it ... So they put Jesus' body there.

Matthew 27:62,65-66 The next day was the holy day after the Preparation Day. And the chief priests and the Pharisees went to talk to Pilate … 'Take some soldiers', Pilate told them. 'Go and make the grave as safe as you can.' So they went and made the grave safe. They fastened the stone across the front with the ruler's seal. Then they left the soldiers there to guard the grave.

Matthew 28:2-4 Then the earth trembled very greatly and one of the Lord's angels came down from heaven. The angel went to the front of the grave. Then he rolled back the stone there and he sat on it. He shone like lightning and his clothes were as white as snow. The guards were so afraid of him that they shook. Then they fell down and became like dead men.

Mark 16:6 He said, 'Do not be so surprised. You are looking for Jesus from Nazareth, whom they killed on a cross. He is not here. He has risen. Look at the place where they laid his body.

Pages 46 and 47

Acts 1:3 After he had suffered, he showed himself to these men. He showed himself to them in many ways. This proved that he was alive. He appeared in front of them many times. This was during a period of 40 days. He talked to them about God's kingdom.

John 3:16 God loved the people in this world so much that he gave his only Son. So everyone who believes in him will never really die. Instead, they will have eternal life.

John 14:1-4 Jesus said to his disciples, 'Do not worry! Trust God. And trust me, too. There are many rooms in my Father's house. I would not tell this to you unless it was true. I am going there to prepare a place for each of you. After I have done this, I will return. And I will take you with me. Then we will all be together in the place where I am. You know the way to the place where I am going.'

Page 48

Acts 1:9-11 After he said this, he returned to heaven. They watched as he went there. A cloud hid him, so then they could not see him. While he went, they were staring up at the sky. Immediately, two men in white clothes stood next to them. They said, 'Men from Galilee, you should not stand here and you should not look at the sky. This Jesus has left you and he has gone up to heaven. But he will come again. He will come in the same way as you have seen him go.'

1 John 5:11-13 This is what God has said. He has given to us eternal life and this life is in his Son. The person who has the Son has this life. But the person who does not have the Son does not have this life. I have written these things to you. You believe in the name of Jesus. You believe that he is the Son of God. You have eternal life. I write so that you may know this.

John 21:25 There were many other things that Jesus did. It would not be possible to write down all these things in books. I think that not even the world itself could contain so many books.

Glossary

Altar: the special platform where they burned animals that people offered to God

Angel: spirits created to serve God

Commandment: a command that God gave; the 10 important commands or rules that God gave to Moses on the mountain of Sinai

Bible: The word means book in the Latin or Greek language

Creation: the act of God in making the world and everything there is; everything that God has made

Cross: two pieces of wood fixed together. The Romans punished people by fixing them to a cross to die. Jesus died this way.

Deceive: to speak what is not true to another person, to lie

Disobey: not obey

Forever: always, never ending

Ghost: a spirit

Gospel: The good news that Jesus came to save us; the four sections in the Bible that tell about the life of Jesus—Matthew, Mark, Luke and John

Heaven: the place where God is; the place of happiness and peace where God lives and rules

Holy: one-of-a-kind, set apart

Lamb: a young sheep

Leprosy: a very bad illness. It is an illness of the skin and bones. Other people would not talk to people who had leprosy. They called them dirty. People with leprosy could not live inside a town. They lived outside the town away from other people.

Lord: a title for God, or Jesus, to show that he is the owner of all things

Punishment: the hurt that comes to a person as a result of their sin

Satan: the name for the worst of the bad spirits that are against God. He has other names: Lucifer (the Shining One) and the Devil. He is the enemy of God.

Saviour: Jesus, the one who saves us; the one who rescues

Sin: to do wrong, bad or evil things; to disobey God; to not follow the rules; the bad things people do

Spirit: the part of us that lives when our body dies; a being, such as an angel, that is always alive, even without a body. There are good spirits, like God's Spirit and his angels. There are also bad spirits, like Satan and his angels.

Trust: to believe something is true; to believe in someone

Yahweh: God's name in the Hebrew language; sometimes called Jehovah

GoodSeed® International

P. O. Box 3704
Olds, AB T4H 1P5
CANADA

Business: 403 556-9955
Facsimile: 403 556-9950
Email: info@goodseed.com

TO ORDER:

Australia	1800 897-333
Canada (English)	800 442-7333
(French)	888 314-3623
Europe	info.eu@goodseed.com
Germany	info.de@goodseed.com
United Kingdom	0800 073-6340
USA	888 654-7333

ORDER ONLINE: goodseed.com

The Story that Matters

Bible verses quoted from the EasyEnglish Bible

Copyright © 2014 by GoodSeed® International

ISBN 978-1-927429-65-5

The Bible verses quoted on pages 56 to 62 were translated into EasyEnglish by Wycliffe Associates (UK). See www.easyenglish.info for specific book-by-book copyright information as well as further details on EasyEnglish.

Printed in the USA • 201407-249-20000

GoodSeed® is a not-for-profit organization that exists for one purpose: *We want to clearly explain the message of the Bible.* **We invite you to contact us if you are interested in ongoing projects or translations.**